"Francis Deng and I worked intensively with the S[...] ment and successive governments in Khartoum fo[...] peace and unity in the Sudan. I know no other [...] much to bridging the gulf that has torn his coun[...] Francis is a strong believer in unity, but one based on equality and justice for all. This book sheds important light on the challenges facing the Sudan and should be taken seriously by all concerned with the developments in the country."—Olusegun Obasanjo, former President of Nigeria

"Over the last several decades, Francis Deng has been one of our major sources of insight into developments in Sudan. I have always been impressed by Deng's ability to analyze the situation compassionately but objectively with a remarkable ability to see the point of view of adversaries. Deng's perspective on his country is an exceptional one that should be given serious attention by all concerned with developments in the Sudan."—Congressman Donald M. Payne, Chairman of the House Sub-Committee on Africa

"This book reflects a penetrating analysis of the problems and a refreshing optimism without which we would be defeated before we even try. I strongly recommend that this book be compulsory reading for all the stakeholders in the peace process in Sudan."—Ibrahim Gambari, Joint Special Representative of the African Union–United Nations Hybrid Operations in Darfur

"Dr. Deng has written a book of extraordinary importance, one that is rich in well-documented information, gives insight beyond any prior publication, and points the way toward practical solutions."—David A. Hamburg, M.D., President Emeritus, Carnegie Corporation of New York

"The continent of Africa and the international community are watching the upcoming referendum in Southern Sudan with grave concern for the future of the country. As Francis Deng explains in this brief overview of the situation, acceptance of the will of the people of the South must be combined with maintaining the aspiration for unity, whatever the outcome of the referendum. Building the foundation for national unity by negotiating post-referendum arrangements is a challenge which the leadership of the Sudan must embrace in earnest and with a lofty vision for the ultimate destiny of the Nation."—Salim Ahmed Salim, President of the Julius Nyerere Foundation

"The title of this book spotlights the challenges confronting the Sudan. This book should act as a catalyst in the debate on these vitally important issues. It is insightful and forward-looking. I hope all Sudanese, Southern and Northern, as well as those concerned about the future of the country and people, will read this book."—Haile Menkerios, Special Representative of the UN Secretary-General in Sudan

"In this readable short book, Francis Deng again lends a reasoned and articulate voice—dispassionate, yet subtly positive—on how the opportunities and challenges facing Sudan can best be tackled in the larger interest."—Taye-Brook Zerihoun, Assistant Secretary-General for Political Affairs, United Nations

"This book is a timely reminder of Francis Deng's lifelong efforts to advance peace and cooperation among Sudanese. It provides a strong basis for dialogue on the future of Sudan and insight on how the country's most challenging questions can be answered."—former President Jimmy Carter, Nobel Peace Laureate

# Sudan at the Brink

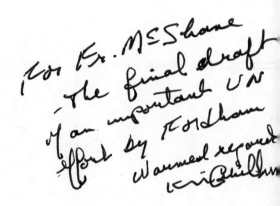

For Fr. MEShane
- The final draft
of an important UN
effort by Fordham
Warmest regards
[signature]

INTERNATIONAL HUMANITARIAN AFFAIRS
Kevin M. Cahill, M.D., series editor

* Available in French translation

# Sudan at the Brink
## Self-Determination and National Unity

**FRANCIS MADING DENG**

A JOINT PUBLICATION OF **FORDHAM UNIVERSITY PRESS** AND
**THE INSTITUTE FOR INTERNATIONAL HUMANITARIAN AFFAIRS**
NEW YORK 2010

Fordham University Press has no responsibility for the
persistence or accuracy of URLs for external or third-
party Internet websites referred to in this publication
and does not guarantee that any content on such
websites is, or will remain, accurate or appropriate.

Fordham University Press also publishes its books in a
variety of electronic formats. Some content that
appears in print may not be available in electronic
books.

Library of Congress Cataloging-in-Publication Data is
available from the publisher.

Printed in the United States of America

12 11 10   5 4 3 2 1
First edition

CONTENTS

Almost fifty years ago, when working as a young physician in the Southern Sudan, I met Francis Deng for the first time. Even then, the region was a war zone. Large numbers of innocent civilians were being killed and maimed and an ancient society was being threatened with destruction; however, I also witnessed the beginnings of the noble, tenacious struggle for understanding, reconciliation, and peace embodied in the life work of Francis Deng. Over the decades I have remained in close contact with Sudan, returning for medical research, humanitarian relief, and training programs. Throughout, Francis Deng has been a wise and steady mentor, helping me to understand the often tortured, and very complex, modern political forces and their effects both North and South.

The eyes of the world are now focused on Sudan not only because of the tragic crisis in the western region of Darfur but also because of the precarious situation unfolding in the southern part of the country. After half a century during which the country experienced two wars between the North and the South (1955–1972 and 1983–2005), the Government of Sudan (GOS) and the Sudan People's Liberation Movement and Army (SPLM/A) concluded the Comprehensive Peace Agreement (CPA) in 2005, the outcome of protracted negotiations in which countries of the region and international partners played a pivotal mediation role.

The Agreement gave the people of the South the right of self-determination to be exercised through a referendum after a six-year interim period during which efforts would be exerted to make the unity option attractive to the South. With only several months left for the referendum in January 2011, it is widely believed that the South will now most likely vote for secession.

Apart from the case of Eritrea, this would make Sudan the first African country to be partitioned, which will be a radical departure from the almost sacrosanct principle of the founding Organization of African Unity and its successor, the African Union, in favor of preserving colonial borders. Eritrean independence from Ethiopia is usually justified on the grounds that it had been a colonial state independent from Ethiopia to which it was later affiliated as a protectorate and into which it was eventually incorporated.

Sudan, geographically the largest country in Africa, carries a special significance for the continent because of its potentially enriching diversity linking sub-Saharan Africa with North Africa and the Middle East, and comprising all the continent's identity factors of race, ethnicity, religion, and culture. It is also a country endowed with abundant natural resources, vital not only to the needs of its own people but also to the region and the wider international community.

Although the recently discovered lucrative oil reserves have attracted the interest of major world consumers and raised the profile of the country internationally, Sudan's vast arable land and plentiful water supplies have long been seen as providing a potential breadbasket for North Africa and the Middle East. The country is rich in livestock, also of great interest to the Middle East, and in minerals, not yet fully explored, and far less exploited.

Sudan is therefore a country in which the stakes are high in opposite directions. As a success story, it can have a positive impact in Africa, the Middle East, and, by extension, the wider international community. In sharp contrast, its fragmentation and failure could have devastating effects internally, regionally, and beyond.

In this brief but comprehensive book, Francis Deng offers a creative analysis of the situation, aimed at addressing, and hopefully resolving, the complex dilemmas confronting Sudan, Africa, and the international community over the critical choice the South will make in January 2011. There is a consensus that the CPA must be faithfully implemented, the referendum credibly conducted, and the choice of the people of the South fully respected.

However, there is grave concern over partitioning the country and the repercussions not only for Sudan, but also the continent of Africa as a whole, and by extension, the global community. Even in material terms, the international community has already invested billions in humanitarian assistance to Sudan, and the United Nations and the African Union maintain two major peacekeeping operations in the South and Darfur. Unless the Southern referendum and results are carefully and constructively managed, the international community could be confronted with yet another crisis with grave humanitarian and fiscal consequences.

This book is a powerful statement by an individual who is deeply concerned about the plight of his people and the destiny of his country, a man who, in many ways, symbolizes the lofty aspirations for unity in which diversity is seen as a source of enrichment and not of destructive conflict, a unity of full equality among all its citizens.

Francis Deng comes from the North-South border area of Abyei in which generations of his forefathers, as Paramount Chiefs, played a pivotal bridging role between the North and the South in partnership with their Missiriya Arab counterparts. His father, the late Chief Deng Majok of the Ngok Dinka, and the Missiriya Arab Chief Babo Nimir are still often referred to as having provided a model of friendly coexistence and cooperation across the racial, ethnic, cultural, and religious divide, a model that the country needs in order to foster sustainable peace and national unity.

Although the Ngok Dinka of Abyei are, by all criteria, Southerners, their area had been administered as part of the North, which gave them a special favorable status during the colonial period. Independence disturbed the delicate balance the British had maintained to the satisfaction of the Dinka. As a reaction to their subordinated and disadvantaged position as a minority among the Arabs, the Ngok Dinka joined their kith and kin in the South in both wars of liberation.

The Abyei Protocol of the CPA gives them the right, through a referendum to be carried out simultaneously with the Southern referendum, to choose to remain in the North or join the South.

Beyond the leadership background of his family, Francis Deng has devoted most of his adult life to the search for peace and unity in his country. He has done this not only in his diplomatic role as his country's Ambassador in several important posts and as Minister of State for Foreign Affairs but also through his scholarly and literary works, reflected in numerous publications. He has served as Representative of the Secretary-General on Internally Displaced Persons for twelve years, and now is Special Advisor of the Secretary-General on the Prevention of Genocide, a position he holds at the level of Under-Secretary General.

This book is an abbreviated testimony of a life-long endeavor, presented with humility and selfless devotion to the cause of peace in Sudan. Francis Deng has been a strong believer in the unity of his country, but one that must be based on the full equality of all its peoples; one to which all Sudanese can feel a sense of belonging with pride and dignity on equal footing; one whose foreign policy serves the interests of the nation by reaching out to African, Arab, Christian, Muslim, and other countries in the global community, for mutually beneficial partnership and cooperation.

Unfortunately, Sudan has so far failed to rise to this lofty vision. If the voters choose unity, it must be implemented in a far more equitable manner than in the past. If they opt for secession, then the process of partition must be as peaceful and harmonious as possible, with both North and South working to establish a framework for close association and cooperation, while leaving open the possibility for reunification, should the right conditions be created.

This is a book that is a must-read for all those concerned with developments in Sudan at this critical juncture in the history of the country. Whatever decision the Sudanese make in the January 2011 referendum, it is imperative that it be an informed choice carefully weighing the implications of secession versus unity. These profound options will likely be debated in the United Nations General Assembly. They will also be carefully considered in multiple other forums where the future of humanitarian action, peacekeeping, and development are considered.

Many people joined forces to enable this book to be available as a central focus for these debates. The President of Fordham University, Rev. Joseph M. McShane, S.J.; Senior Vice President/Chief Academic Officer Stephen Freedman; and the Dean of the Graduate School of Arts and Sciences, Nancy Busch, each deserve my deep gratitude for their commitment to its rapid production. Mr. Fredric Nachbaur, Director of Fordham University Press, and his staff devoted weekends, nights, and their professional skills to assure that the book would be available in time for a timely debate within the African Union and other concerned circles. Finally, I wish to acknowledge Brendan Cahill and the staff of the Institute for International Humanitarian Affairs (IIHA) at Fordham University.

Sudan at the Brink is the ninth volume in the IIHA book series, and is an important contribution to our extensive teaching programs. This book has been generously supported by The Center for International Humanitarian Cooperation.

Kevin M. Cahill, M.D.
University Professor and Director
The Institute for International Humanitarian Affairs
Fordham University

# Sudan at the Brink

After years of protracted negotiations, with regional and international mediation, the Government of Sudan and the Sudan People's Liberation Movement and Army (SPLM/A) concluded the Comprehensive Peace Agreement (CPA). The settlement met with varying responses at home and abroad. Southerners responded with jubilation primarily because the agreement granted them the right of self-determination to be exercised after a six-year interim period through a referendum that would offer a choice between unity and secession. Northerners generally felt that the CPA had given the South too much by granting them full autonomy and significant participation in the Government of National Unity as well as an independence option after six years. The international community was relieved that the war that had raged intermittently for half a century had, at long last, come to an end. While the potential partition of the country remained a matter of concern, the stipulation that efforts would be exerted to make unity an attractive option for the South provided ground for optimism that Sudan would survive as a united nation.

Perhaps because of the ambivalences over the agreement, viewed by both sides as more the result of external pressures than a free expression of the national will, the implementation of the CPA has been fraught with difficulties and controversies. The opposition parties in the North that had been excluded in the negotiations have been antagonistic to the agreement. Even members of the ruling National

Congress Party (NCP) that had negotiated the agreement have not been unified in their acceptance of the CPA. The three border areas of Abyei, Blue Nile, and Southern Kordofan, which had been the subjects of special protocols, pose their own challenges, poised as they are between the North and the South.

The protocol on Abyei gave the people the right to decide in a referendum, to be exercised simultaneously with the Southern referendum, whether to remain part of the North or join the South. But differences persisted over the borders of the area, initially determined by the Abyei Border Commission (ABC) whose findings the NCP-dominated government rejected on the grounds that the ABC had exceeded its mandate. The dispute was later adjudicated by a special arbitration tribunal at The Hague, whose decision has not been implemented. Often referred to ironically as the oil-rich area of Abyei, the area shows no evidence of oil wealth and the 2 percent of the revenue from the oil produced in the area, which the Abyei Protocol allocates to the area, has not been made available to the people of Abyei, and the amount required to be transferred to the Abyei Administration under the regular national budget remains in question. The protocol on the other two areas calls for popular consultation to decide whether the special arrangements under the CPA are acceptable to the people. Vague as it is, this provision raised its own controversies and conflicting interpretations, ranging from degrees of self-administration within the North to a choice between remaining part of the North and joining the South.

An aspect of the problems of the CPA implementation was the complicating Darfur crisis. While the negotiations of the CPA were underway and had reached critical points, the international community feared that Darfur might be a distraction and therefore tended to give it a lower priority. With the CPA concluded and the crisis in Darfur escalating into a tragedy of grave magnitude, attention shifted to Darfur and the CPA became relegated to a lower priority. Even the Oslo pledges of support that would take peace dividends to the South were never honored.

All in all, while peace was precariously maintained under the CPA, the implementation of its various provisions relating to power sharing, wealth sharing, security arrangements, census, border demarcation, and the conduct of mid-term elections proved to be very contentious, reflecting deep mistrust between the parties in the agreement. For the South, the challenge became how to protect the CPA from collapsing and depriving the people of the South of their most precious achievement under the agreement—the exercise of the right of self-determination. The North appeared ambivalently poised between resisting and eroding those elements of the agreement that favored the South and avoiding a return to war. Most observers seemed convinced that the NCP would not honor the right of self-determination for the South, despite rhetorical statements by the leadership to the contrary.

Ironically, although the preservation of unity was considered of paramount importance, especially to the North, not enough was being done to make unity attractive to the South. This raised suspicions in certain circles, including in the North, that the NCP in fact favored Southern secession to rid themselves of the non-Muslim factor that was a constraint in their implementation of the Arab-Islamic agenda. Cynics believed that the NCP was not concerned about secession because they did not intend to honor the self-determination provisions any way.

As the interim period was approaching its end, the African region and the international community began to take more seriously the possible implications of the Southern exercise of self-determination. The more the international community demonstrated the resolve to support the full implementation of the CPA, including the holding of the self-determination referendum within the agreed timetable, and as it became quite evident that unity had not been made attractive and that secession seemed to be the most likely outcome, the more apprehensions about the negative implications of partitioning the country began to receive greater attention and concerns.

Some leading regional and international personalities began to question the wisdom of allowing Southern secession, which began to be viewed as a potential disaster for the South itself, Sudan as a whole, the East African region, and the continent of Africa. The alarm bells were very much in tune with what the North had always argued—that the South was not capable of independence; that without the uniting conflict with the North, intertribal warfare would tear the region apart and create chaos that would endanger not only Sudan, but the entire region. And indeed, the mounting tribal conflicts in the South, which Southerners attributed, at least in part, to Northern machinations, proved to be a self-fulfilling prophecy by the North. Some well-intentioned African leaders even adopted a revisionist criticism of the self-determination provisions of the CPA as a bad example for Africa, as it would open a Pandora's box of secessionist movements on the continent.

With the January 2011 self-determination referendum fast approaching, the debate over the prospects of unity intensified. Ironically, Khartoum also began to generate a campaign throughout the country in the belated effort to promote the cause of unity. The government began to initiate development projects in the South in an attempt to make unity attractive. While it would seem too late for such efforts to have a significant impact on the position of most Southerners, it is not too late to debate the merits of unity and whether self-determination is reconcilable with the preservation of national unity.

This book aims at contributing to that debate by reconceptualizing unity to remain an ongoing goal, whatever the outcome of the 2011 referendum in the South. Whatever the decision of the South on the issue of unity or secession, the two parts of the country will remain in the same geographical proximity, will continue to interact, and, in varying ways, will become even more interdependent than they have been. All this means that there will undoubtedly be significant elements of unity beyond partition. Unity and partition represent degrees of relationship. The challenge for the North and the South is to work out the arrangements that will reconcile partition with ongoing challenges of unity.

Following this introduction, the book begins with a brief overview of the situation with a focus on aspirations for national unity. This is followed by two statements on the pertinent themes: First a 1989 address to the Dialogue on Peace Issues convened by the nascent Revolution for National Salvation that had seized power three months earlier, and then a 2009 keynote address to a symposium cosponsored by the United Nations Mission in Sudan (UNMIS) on Self-determination and National Unity. These statements are then followed by a note on the situation that I wrote shortly after my return from the symposium. Since negotiations pose ongoing challenges for addressing the myriad conflicts in Sudan, I have included a chapter entitled "Ten Principles on Negotiation." The book ends with a brief conclusion that places an optimistic emphasis on the vision of a New Sudan as a common ground for forging unity, even beyond possible partition through the referendum.

Needless to say, I have prepared this book in my personal capacity and not as the Special Adviser of the UN Secretary-General on the Prevention of Genocide. Accordingly, the views expressed in the book are entirely mine and are not necessarily shared by the Secretary-General or the United Nations, nor do they reflect the position of the publishers.

# 1 | Aspirations for National Unity

The 2005 Comprehensive Peace Agreement (CPA) between the Government of the Sudan (GOS) and the Sudan People's Liberation Movement and Army (SPLM/A) gives the South the right to secede, but it also stipulates that all efforts be exerted during the six-year interim period to make unity an attractive option for the South. The implication of this stipulation is that the burden of making unity attractive lies with the North. The overwhelming view in the South is that the pursuit of a rigid view of unity has already cost the country as a whole and the South in particular too much in terms of lives lost, physical destruction, and retarded development. A more flexible and constructive understanding of unity and how to achieve it is urgently called for.

Of course, it is easy to see that the North, which has dominated the unity framework as conventionally understood, would want to sustain that framework, with all it offers in terms of control over power, wealth, services, development opportunities, and the definition of the country as Arab and Islamic. But this framework has been challenged from the start and, since independence, liberation movements have violently resisted the status quo. It would not be surprising if indeed a significant faction of the Northern Arab-Islamic elite that is in control of the State now sees the South as a distraction from the Northern monolithic vision of Sudan as Arab and Islamic. From this perspective, Southern secession might be viewed as a relief. However, to complicate the picture even more, there are Northern factions who, though sharing the conventional vision of Sudan as Arab and Islamic, contest the revivalist version of the ruling National Congress Party (NCP) of Islam and their monopoly of power and the national resources. These opposition groups would want to use the South as a tool for changing the regime, a practice that has characterized regime change since independence. Then there are those who genuinely believe in a secular, more African-oriented Sudan, for whom the South is a natural ally. These groups, by no means confined to the non-Arab marginalized regions, would see secession as a major weakening for the opposition's power base and capacity to overturn the system or pressure for inclusive reform.

On the part of the South the most obvious preference for the vast majority is secession and the formation of an independent African secular state. That was the objective of the first war of liberation (1955–1972). The declared objective of the second war (1983–2005) was, however, the liberation of the whole Sudan and the creation of a New Sudan of full equality, without discrimination on the grounds of race, ethnicity, religion, culture or gender. This vision was initially resisted within the SPLM/A, generating a violent conflict between the separatists and the unionists. It then became ambivalently accepted in the South as a clever ploy by the leader of the SPLM/A, Dr. John Garang, to neutralize antisecessionist sentiment in the country, in Africa, and in the international community, and to win support for the lofty principles of justice and equality. The dominant groups in the North saw it as naive, presumptuous and offensive to the established Arab-Islamic national identity. With time, it increasingly gained popular acceptance, especially among the marginalized, non-Arab regions of the North—the Nuba Mountains, Blue Nile, the Beja, and Darfur, all of whom took up arms in a chain of interconnected regional rebellions. Even the Nubians to the far north embraced the call for the New Sudan, and indeed take pride in their pre-Islamic African civilization of the Nile Valley.

The vision of the New Sudan aimed at correcting two historic distortions associated with the Old Sudan. One is the self-perception of the dominant Arabized groups at the Center, who, despite being an African-Arab hybrid with the African elements more visibly pronounced, view themselves as Arab—racially, ethnically, and culturally—with Islam as an augmenting ingredient and to the neglect, and even disdain, of their African element. The other distortion is the projection of this distorted self-perception as the identity framework for the whole nation, notwithstanding the racial, ethnic, cultural, and religious diversity of the country. Social scientists maintain that what matters the most in determining identity is what you think you are and not what you objectively are. That would be acceptable if self-perceptions did not impact negatively on others. In the case of Sudan, distorted self-perceptions have been the bases for discrimination, marginalization, exclusion, and denial of fundamental rights and civil liberties to groups that constitute the majority of the peoples of the country. In the interest of sustainable peace and national unity, these divisive myths should be corrected and the common ground explored and consolidated. This can be considered the win-win approach, since it denies neither the African nor the Arab element.

Initially, the Sudanese and the outside world saw Sudan simplistically as a dualism between the Arab-Muslim North and the African South, comprising adherents of traditional beliefs and modern converts to Christianity, even though the overwhelming majority of the peoples of the North are non-Arab, though Muslim. British colonialism developed the North, especially the Arab Center, economically and politically, and neglected the South; neglected also were the peripheral non-Arab regions of the North, which were subsumed into the Arab-Muslim identity of the North that gave them a false sense of superiority by association. Sudan's independence for the South essentially meant the Arabs taking over from the British in a form of internal colonialism, triggering the first war, which ended with the Addis Ababa Agreement that granted the South regional autonomy. The unilateral abrogation of that agreement ten years later triggered the second war that postulated the vision of a New United Sudan and ended with the CPA.

Although it continued to be viewed as primarily the brainchild of Dr. John Garang, the vision of the New Sudan provided the SPLM/A with a powerful motif that became the centerpiece of the morale-boosting war songs of the Movement. The essence of the message these songs conveyed was that the indigenous people of Sudan were reclaiming their country as a whole, North and South, and that those who identified themselves as Arabs must return to their homeland abroad. Autonomy was rejected as a compromise that surrendered the whole country.

Of course, the leadership articulated this message in a more sophisticated language of inclusivity and equality, without discrimination on any ground. The sense of pride in their African identity which the South projected to the nation began to awaken African consciousness in the marginalized non-Arab regions of the North. As the message became increasingly inspiring to these regions, the vision of a New Sudan became credibly threatening to the Arab Center. The Muslim Brothers, who metamorphosed several times in their quest for power, their latest political identity being the ruling NCP, used Islamic revivalism as a mobilizing tool in a holy war (jihad) against the infidels in the South and anti-Islamic secularists in the North. The war intensified into a zero-sum conflict of identities not only between the North and the South but also within the North.

Amidst the travails of the downfall of the Ethiopian strongman Mengistu Haile Mariam, who had been a staunch supporter of the SPLM/A, the Movement became once more violently divided between the dissident commanders, who fell back on the erstwhile objective of self-determination for the South with the aim of full independence, and the dominant group that remained committed to the New Sudan vision. Although the latter prevailed, the principle of self-determination, which had been a unifying objective of Southern struggle since independence, provided ground for compromise between the adversaries and became a centerpiece in the SPLM/A's negotiations with the government several years later. Although making unity attractive was stipulated as a viable challenge to secession, five years after the CPA was concluded, the general consensus in 2009 was that unity had not been made attractive and that the South was most likely to vote for independence in the 2011 self-determination referendum.

A missing link in this equation is John Garang, the principal proponent and champion of the New Sudan vision, whose accidental death in a helicopter crash, only two weeks after being sworn in as First Vice President of the Republic and President of the Government of Southern Sudan, shocked Sudan, Africa, and the concerned world.

The way he had been received in Khartoum by crowds estimated in the millions from all over Sudan on his return after over twenty years leading the liberation struggle in the jungle, represented a credible threat to the adherents of the Old Sudan. And indeed, had John Garang lived, there is strong evidence that his leadership would have transcended the North-South divide and he could have been a formidable challenger to El-Bashir for the presidency. And if he had won the presidency, he would have effectively used his New Sudan agenda to rally forces across the nation and advanced the cause of democratic transformation of the governance system as envisaged in the CPA.

But John Garang is gone and the question now is: What choices does Sudan still have? Unity, desirable as it is, can only be achieved and sustained in a Sudan that accommodates its diversities within a framework of equality, without discrimination on the grounds of race, ethnicity, religion, culture, and gender. That is the New Sudan vision. But that vision cannot be acceptable to those ideologically committed to the Arab-Islamic identity and agenda for the nation. That is the position of the ruling NCP, a reincarnation of the National Islamic Front and its forerunners, the National Islamic Charter and the Muslim Brotherhood.

The liberal elements in the North would want the South, in particular the SPLM/A, to continue to champion the cause of unity in a New Sudan. For all those who want Sudan to remain united, that is, of course, a noble vision, not unlike the New South Africa—championed by the African National Congress (ANC) under the wise leadership of Nelson Mandela—which all recognize as a noble vision. But it is one that would require the South to continue to sacrifice in the struggle for a lofty, but elusive national objective; and for the NCP to also embrace transformation.

In fairness to the North, it is difficult to see how the South could have gained so much in the struggle without the support of the Nuba and the Ingassana (Funj), who joined the SPLM/A in the mid-1980s, and even those who struggled outside the Movement.

The Sudanese now have critical choices to make. Continuing in a united Sudan under the old order is clearly unacceptable, not only to the South, but also to the non-Arab areas of the North. Full implementation of the CPA is the most credible and peaceful way forward for the South. As already noted, it is now widely expected that the self-determination referendum is likely to lead to secession as the Southern choice. In the marginalized non-Arab regions of the North—the Nuba, the Ingassana (Funj), the Beja, the Darfurians, and the Nubians in the far North, which remain disgruntled in the Old Sudan—the struggle for equality in a New Sudan will continue and the Northern regional liberation movements will look to the South for support. Southern support would in turn most likely trigger Northern manipulation of ethnic differences in the South to undermine its stability and independence. Hence, even though the two nations would be separated politically, the reach that each would maintain into the other would persist, perhaps leading to even greater instability than under the current status quo.

All this calls for consensus building among the major political forces in the country. Whether the country remains united or gets divided, the unity scenario would require a framework of genuine autonomy for all the regions (with or without the South) to be self-governing and to have an equitable share in the government of national unity, with a fair distribution of power, wealth, services, and development opportunities. The separatist scenario (for the South) would require a framework of friendly partition between the North and the South, an equitable post-referendum sharing of natural resources, in particular oil revenues, open borders and guaranteeing freedom of movement, residence, employment, and choice of citizenship. Most importantly, the South and North would remain key components in a broader process of regional economic and political integration, which is indeed a bigger challenge than the immediate issue of the referendum, and one that is part and parcel of the historic march towards African unity.

# 2 | Dialogue on Peace Issues

In September, 1989, less than three months after the alliance between the National Islamic Front and Islamist elements in the Sudanese army seized power on June 30, 1989, in the name of the Revolution for National Salvation, Bona Malwal and I went to Addis Ababa to confer with Dr. John Garang de Mabior, leader of Sudan People's Liberation Movement and Army (SPLM/A), on the developments in the country and the region. In accordance with my principle of maintaining contact with all the parties, I decided to proceed to Khartoum after our visit to Addis Ababa in order to meet and consult with the new leaders. My decision was strongly opposed by relatives and friends, but I insisted on going. As I did not know how I would be received, I was very nicely surprised by the warm reception accorded me. Through the good offices of Colonel Martin Machwei Malwal, one of the three Southerners in the Revolution Command Council, I met with General Omar Hassan Al-Beshir, the leader of the revolution, and virtually all the members of the Revolution Command Council. At my request, I was even granted permission to visit members of the previous government who were then detained at the Kober prison, including Sayed Sadiq al-Mahdi, Sayed Mohamed Osman al-Mirghani, and Dr. Hassan al-Turabi, who ironically later emerged as the spiritual leader of the revolution.

I arrived in Khartoum as the National Dialogue on Peace Issues was being convened and I was informed that an invitation was about to be sent to me in Washington to participate in the deliberations. As I had to rush back to duties in the United States, I could not stay, but I was asked to address the conference. Although I explained that I was there to learn and had not yet acquired enough insight to make a statement, Colonel Martin Malwal and his colleagues urged me to speak, lest my silence be misconstrued as opposition. In accepting the invitation, I decided to speak the truth as I saw it, politely but firmly. What follows is a transcript of my tape-recorded statement to the conference.

Both the substance and the tone of the statement should be understood in the context of the timing, an initial phase of less than three months into the nascent revolution, whose colors and policies were controversially Islamic but as yet not crystallized. I should also say that at the time, the SPLM/A was still united behind the goal of a New Sudan. It was not until the split of Riek Machar, Lam Akol, and Gordon Kong in August 1991 that the separatist trend emerged in glaring light. The demand for self-determination, which later became a point of consensus in the South, came even later. Nor has the SPLM/A abandoned its call for a new, democratically restructured Sudan. What might have become more crystallized is that as a result of the CPA, the South is now granted the right of self-determination to be exercised through a referendum that includes the right to secede, but only after efforts have been exerted to make unity an attractive option for the South.

I, for one, have always seen three available options: unity on the basis of a new, fundamentally restructured Sudan; some form of loose coexistence that will try to reconcile unity with separatism; and outright partition. I should say, however, that the crisis of national identity, which has been a subject of considerable attention in recent years, will persist, whatever option is adopted. In view of its composition, especially in terms of the Arab-African dualism, even if the South were to separate, the North would still have to reckon with the crisis of its own identity. And given the considerable numbers of Northerners of Southern origins—who have in varying degrees remained in the closet, but are bound to be attracted to come out should the South succeed in projecting a more recognized and respectable profile—even separation is not likely to diminish entirely the bonds of kinship and cultural affinities that link the two parts of the country, but which prolonged animosity has tended to overshadow. More serious thought will therefore need to be given to the relationship than Sudanese on both sides generally tend to do. It is perhaps in this spirit that the message of what is required to develop and consolidate a uniting national identity framework should be an important element in the ongoing debate about the future of the country, even beyond the

Southern referendum. The notion of unity beyond partition becomes relevant in this context.

This was the essence of my statement to the National Dialogue on Peace Issues in Khartoum, September 1989. I have reproduced the transcripts in sections with substantive subheadings to facilitate the flow for the reader and to provide coherence for the statement in the context of the search for peace and unity in the country.

## Appreciation for the Warm Reception

I would like to say at the beginning of my remarks how appreciative I am to have come on what was a passing visit to find myself invited, not only to participate in the discussions of the conference in general, but also to be given the opportunity to address this gathering at this stage in your deliberations. This is particularly the case because I have to rush back to duties in the United States, and therefore will not be here to participate in the work of the conference. I should also say and stress what I have had occasion to say to the media: my purpose for coming here was dualistic in nature. One was in line with the work I do at the Brookings Institution, as someone entrusted with the establishment of an African studies program, which had not been there before. But by virtue of being Sudanese, I am also interested in the affairs of my country and have made studying the problems of Sudan part of my occupational priorities. Therefore, my intention was, in view of the changes that our country has undergone recently, to come and acquaint myself with the developments, to talk with the leaders of the Revolution for National Salvation as well as to ordinary citizens, to observe the situation in order to enlighten myself and be better equipped to carry on both my research on the various aspects of nation-building in our country and my own efforts in the ongoing search for peace.

I got a lot more from this visit than I had expected in that I have been very warmly received and have learned a great deal already. Leaders of the Revolution have opened their doors and their hearts, to put me in the picture as to their thinking and the efforts being exerted. I can say that I am much wiser by virtue of the few days I have spent here than I was when I arrived. It is with this background that I am particularly appreciative of the opportunity to be a party to this historic moment.

The search for peace is a challenge for all of us Sudanese, wherever we may be, whether we are in the government, outside the government, or even outside the country. Knowing the Sudanese as we do, I think we have to assume that unless proven otherwise, every Sudanese is committed to the interests of the country, and to contributing whatever he or she can to the realization of national objectives and, in particular, the cause of peace and unity.

## A Personal Perspective on Unity

Speaking of the cause of peace and unity, let me beg your indulgence to say a personal word about what this means to me. To me, the unity of Sudan is not simply a question of personal reflection or decision based on some information I have gathered in the course of my education and interaction with other Sudanese; it is a deep-rooted conviction, an act of faith that goes back to my background. Without making these national issues too personal, I am not ashamed to say that it goes even to the legacy of my family. I come from the North-South border area of Abyei and from a family which for generations has led the cause of positive peaceful interaction between different peoples of Sudan, north and south, Arabs and Dinkas, fostering a sense of togetherness and cooperation in the promotion of mutual interests in that sensitive North-South crossroads. To some extent, their efforts fed in a very small but significant way into the larger picture of national unity.

I am sure that some of you, if not many, will have heard of names of people like the late Nazir Deng Majok, my father, who, together with his friend and neighbor, the late Nazir Babo Nimir of the Missiriya Arabs, maintained peace and stability in an area of immense sensitivity and volatility, where pastoral tribes come into contact, interact, and, not infrequently, threaten explosions of conflicts. Although we tend to not really see how these individuals in their different ways contributed to the building of our nation and to the stability of the country at its roots, I believe they have given the nation a foundation that we should look to with serious consideration.

Maybe because of this personal background, or because of my academic interests, which began with the study of law, but became increasingly historical, anthropological, and sociological, I have seen it fit to learn from these experiences and they have reinforced my vision for the nation. Indeed, I can claim that part of my academic preoccupation, which has been fostered by my own career not only at home but also abroad, has had to do with such studies. Some of you will have seen the two books: *Recollections of Babo Nimir* and *The Man Called Deng Majok*, which in essence reflect that contribution of leadership at the grassroots. So, when I speak of national unity, I mean it in a very deep and personal sense that goes back to my roots and to generations in my family.

## The SPLM/A Perspective on Unity

With that personal note, let me now go to what I am sure is an important consideration in your minds, and that is, how our brothers and sisters on the other side see the cause of unity. By those brothers, I mean of course, those in the SPLM/A. We often hear the question posed, "What does John Garang want?" Sometimes, the question is broadened to, "What does the SPLM/A want?" Their views have been articulated in a number of ways, in documents, and even in books, and it is certainly not for me to speak for them. But the mere fact that the question is posed means that whatever they have said to explain their point of view, the message has not been heeded. As some of you know, I have been involved in the peace process, trying to facilitate communication between the different parties, while also doing more than simply being a messenger, in the hope of fostering a common ground and narrowing the gap. From this standpoint, I believe I can venture some observations on what it is I understand our brothers who have taken up arms to be fighting for.

I really believe that at least insofar as our brother, John Garang, the leader of the movement, is concerned (and I should say that I have conducted extensive discussions with him), there can be no doubt about his commitment to national unity. I am profoundly convinced about this. I am sure it will come as a surprise to many that there is no hidden agenda. Many believe that the talk about the unity of the country is a tactical or even strategic framework within which other, more limited regional objectives might be pursued. Let me go beyond the individual, brother John Garang, and tell you something about what I believe is a broader-based commitment to unity. Again, going back to my scholarly interests, I should say that I have of late been listening very intensely to the war songs of the SPLM/A. I know that many of my colleagues, lawyers, political scientists, and others probably think that these traditional sources of information can be dismissed as not particularly useful to understanding the core issues of war and peace. But if one knows something about the function of songs in traditional society and if one also knows something about the extent to which SPLA has built on some of the traditional cultural values and practices, one will know that songs are a very important source of individual and collective expression of consciousness. War songs may be composed by poets and therefore can be labeled as individual, but they express shared experiences and are therefore collective. Even the process of their composition is usually the result of consultations among the members of the identified group, an age-set, a regiment, or a battalion. And by virtue of their being used as songs of morale-uplifting under conditions of warfare, these become, whether as starting points or as end results, expressions of collective consciousness. I have observed in the songs of the SPLA, and I have listened very intensely, a tremendous shift in the outlook of the fighting men and women, most of whom are Southerners.

In the past, Southerners were generally known to be fighting in pursuit of regional aspirations. Their expectations could be met by arrangements that would give them effective control at the regional level. That was what was achieved under the Addis Ababa Accord. In these songs, both in words and in spirit, I sense a strategic shift toward a national vision. This vision is no longer talking about the land of the South, as defined by earlier boundaries; it is talking about the country as a whole. And in talking about the country, these songs are identifying the Sudanese not by the labels of the past that were limited, but by new criteria that accommodate every Sudanese as a brother and a sister. And behind these words and the spirit the songs express, there is a sense of empowerment, of confidence, indeed of destiny. They believe that they will achieve these national objectives.

Another feature of these songs, which I find quite remarkable, is the alternation from tribal languages into Arabic and back. Sometimes, the song begins with an Arabic sentence and quickly goes into a local language, and sometimes, without any warning, it falls back into Arabic. Sometimes, the song may all be in Arabic. Sometimes, sentence by sentence, it alternates, or a word is stuck in somewhere. The words stuck in might be local or Arabic. What I come back with is the dynamics of the Sudanese perceptions of those words, as an aspect of the shared culture, whether we are talking ethnically, culturally or linguistically. In a sense, the reality of Sudan is being expressed in a modest but significant symbolic form. Again, I believe the Southerner has shifted his vision, has freed himself from the local biases that had to do with language and is looking in a dynamic way toward a national vision that accommodates diversities, even if the language included there is not the most representative in terms of conventional forms.

What does one conclude from these features of the SPLA reflections, whether in their writings, speeches, or songs? I believe it means that there has been a dramatic shift that we have to take much more seriously than we seem to do when we speak of whether the problem should be defined as southern, regional, or national. When we hear of the differences of opinion on whether we are discussing a southern problem or a national problem, I feel convinced that it is not a matter of semantics; I think it is a matter of strategic vision of the problem. Depending on how you perceive it, your approach, your analysis, your conclusions and therefore your solutions, will be influenced very profoundly. I would submit that the strategic shift from looking at the problem as a local southern problem to viewing it as a national problem has profound implications. It is very significant to the policies we adopt and the kinds of solutions we are developing. It may well be that whichever way we begin our analysis, or wherever our perspective starts, we would probably end up seeing the whole picture because, even if the problem were viewed as regional, its impact has become national. But I think viewing it as regional or national has its special implications.

## The SPLM/A Challenge to the Nation

What I have just said tells us several things, both positive and negative, about the challenge facing us. In the positive direction, I think it is important to realize that we have gone a long way in conceptualizing and working toward national unity. I think it is a major development that we do not hear separatism as part of the Southern agenda. And that means that we have unified at least our vision in favor of national unity. This certainly is positive. The negative is that the vision coming from the SPLM/A is one that is threatening to the establishment because it is challenging us to have a fundamental reexamination of our vision for our country and its future. When I speak of the vision coming from the SPLM/A, I really want to emphasize that what we hear, whether it is in their writings or in their songs, and what we know about the nature of the conflict and who is fighting the war in the south, all indicate that we should not see the leadership in isolation from the masses. The leadership is heading a much more broad-based movement which is reflective of an explosion involving many, many young people from high schools and universities who, as a result of a long experience with deep-rooted grievances, have despaired and have resorted to the use of arms. This is the result of a situation in which they did not see any promising peaceful alternatives. These people live under conditions which are not easy, to say the least; but, frankly, those with whom I have come in touch during my visits to Addis Ababa see a new sense of fulfillment in their own struggle, a sense of dignity in their fighting for something they believe in, sacrificing much for their convictions. It is important to emphasize that the enormous energies of hundreds of thousands of young people who constitute a potential source of reconstruction are being used for destruction because this is the only way they find to express their dignity.

What does this mean? It means that there is definitely a threat to the established way of doing things. When a people take up arms and say that talking has produced no result, it means that they have despaired and have given up hope in the peaceful solutions to the problems. Southerners have taken up arms with a vision aimed at revising the character of the nation. Their orientation is that only by changing the system at the national level can they guarantee meaningful fulfillment of their aspirations at the regional level. They are already posing a threat, a real challenge. That is why one comes across many Northern Sudanese, men of goodwill, even people who are otherwise liberal and open-minded, who would suddenly pose the rhetorical question: Whom is Garang coming to liberate? Or whom does he expect to rule? There is something deeply divisive in saying: Whom is so-and-so coming to rule? But the threat is a reaction coming from those forces that are decidedly committed to changing the character of our nation.

If we take these two positions together: the positive in terms of the commitment to national unity and the negative in terms of the threat to the established order of things, what we get is a challenge that calls on our leaders to fundamentally recognize the problem and the need for new solutions, what the leaders of the Revolution for National Salvation have been calling a radical solution. Given the common vision that is articulated in the statements of the SPLM/A and what we have now heard of the statement by the leaders of the Revolution for National Salvation, it seems to me that these two factors, the positive and the negative, could be reconciled. We could rise above the confrontation that comes from a reaction to a threat, to one of a common vision and a common stand in fostering the kind of Sudan with which we can all identify.

## Issues for the National Dialogue

Let me now address some of the issues that are being contested. In all the efforts that we have gone through in the search for peace, certain issues have been identified and people are in agreement that these are the issues that are divisive. I will not go over them in any detail, other than to mention them briefly: The divisive issues include power-sharing, sharing of resources or national wealth, the nature of government and the state, the relationship between religion and the state, problems of national identity, and issues pertaining to foreign policy. Perhaps the most critical factor that has been at the core of the discussion so far is the question of religion. Related to this question is the issue of identity, which touches not only on ethnicity, but also on culture and national identification. I think it is fair to say that the emphasis that has been given to religion has tended to oversimplify a very complex picture. It is in the nature of religion that it is very sensitive and goes to the core of matters of identity.

When we speak of the relationship between religion and the state, we are talking of religion as a symbol of the larger picture which may determine issues of one's identity and the identity of the nation. This includes issues of who occupies what position in the country or in the society, as well as issues of how the sharing of power and even resources can be affected by religious identification. It is only by bearing in mind that religion has become a symbol of something much larger that we can avoid oversimplifying the problem when we characterize religion as the core factor in this complex situation. In looking at the question of religion we have to bear in mind a number of complex and interconnected issues. As long as we make one religion the basis for defining our identity and the identity of the nation, and for determining who occupies what position in the hierarchy of power and the sharing of resources, there can be no question that full equality of religions and of individuals and groups belonging to different religions cannot be achieved. And as long as there is no full equality between citizens, there can be no viable peace, for such a system would relegate certain groups to a secondary or tertiary position by virtue of their religious affiliation.

On the other hand, to the extent that religion tells its adherents that there is no separation between religion and the state, to demand that they must adhere to a different perception of the relationship between religion and the state is to question fundamentally their religious beliefs and rights. Such a demand is bound to provoke a reaction that can be threatening to mutual accommodation. Here, we have a dilemma. On the one hand, it is necessary to affirm the equality of citizens in full identification with the nation, to ensure their equal participation in the power process and in the sharing of resources without discrimination based on religion. On the other hand, there is the competing need to ensure the freedom to realize one's religious ideals as one sees fit, and if the relationship between religion and the state is part of those ideals, then one has the right not to be required to deviate from the tenets of one's faith.

Frankly, it is a very difficult position. But I think it is a situation that calls for reassessment of priorities. It is one that forces us to ask ourselves: What is the hierarchy of priorities as we see them? Is the form or the letter of what my religion tells me the one that should guide me as a top priority? Or are mutual accommodation and the building of the nation together on the basis of full equality the top priority? Some people believe in the first. I have had occasion to talk to someone who takes that position. It was a long discussion that ended with him emphasizing, with full respect for my views, that he fully understood the point of view of the non-Muslims, that as a Muslim his religion tells him there can be no separation between religion and the state, and of course there was no question in his mind that his religion came first.

With due deference to arguments to the contrary, his priority was clearly religious and he made it emphatically clear that his religion was more important than his nation. That may well be one man's point of view. Others may say that while my religion is more important than my nation, I can also reconcile the principles of my religion with the principles of my nation and thereby remove the conflict. But there are those who may say that these positions are irreconcilable, in which case, unfortunately, we have the war of wills and the tragedy will continue until it is resolved in one way or another. But I really think the vast majority of the Sudanese people believe in the unity of our nation as the top priority. Unity as a matter of principle is desirable; it is a source of mutual enrichment, strength, and security. Disunity poses serious threats. Quite apart from the fact that partitioning countries is not desirable in the world we live in today, there are also pragmatic reasons for why going our separate ways is a threat to our mutual security. If, therefore, the unity of our nation is our priority, and bearing in mind the need to respect our respective values and religions, is it possible for us to find a ground for reconciling these considerations? I submit that we can look to our experiences of times past to see whether we were any less religious when we followed alternative arrangements, and therefore whether those experiences can help us in building the future. We can look to the experiences of others and see how these experiences and the methods and strategies adopted by those others can help us reconcile our differences. I believe that where there is a common will to build a united nation, there will be a way to reconcile the differences.

Coming to the question of identity, which, as I said, is closely associated also with religion and culture, it has been my personal conviction as a result of academic and scholarly pursuits, that, for reasons of history, we have tended to build our identities and perceptions of who we are as a people and as a nation on myths. Those myths have evolved over a long period, during which we have been subjected to a hierarchy of statuses based on ethnicity, race, culture, language, and religion. We have been made to believe that being this is inferior, being that is superior, and being that is even better. And also being allowed relatively to pass from being one to the other, in a flexible process, we have tended to define our concepts of who we are in a way that might have been psychologically gratifying to us, but is not so much based on the realities of what we are, as on what we have been molded to believe we are. Frankly, one of those concepts is the way we identify ourselves as Arabs, Africans, or Blacks. There is certainly an element of truth in all of those because otherwise they would not persist. But there is a certain element of distortion and exaggeration in those labels that divide us. In a way, myths become realities, but myths are the result of the molding of realties, and it is a process that continues according to one's priorities. If I am given a system that permits me to identify myself liberally, with whatever gives me a sense of dignity and enhancement of status, of course I will identify with that which promotes my status. That is fine as long as it does not create problems for others. I mean, if we were in a country where we could all identify ourselves as Arabs or Muslims and have no problems of diversity that threaten to divide us, there would be no problem. The crisis comes in when what we identify ourselves and our nation to be becomes divisive in a way that then threatens the unity of the nation we want to build.

It has been my policy-oriented assumption that the labels that divide us are the result of myths that stratified our races, cultures, languages, and religions. If we were to remove those myths, we would uncover the realities that remain and still unite all the Sudanese. We all take pride when we are outside Sudan in being Sudanese, and we quickly discover the elements that make us Sudanese. It is only when we come to our narrow context that we are blinded by these myths that give us status, but have also tended to divide us.

Lest I be misunderstood, it is not my argument that by removing the myths that divide the Sudanese, we are obliterating, dismissing, or disregarding those elements of identity that have been part of our mixed identities. As I have said, myth in itself has accommodated or embodied realities so that it is part of our realities. But if we put our house in order and we are comfortable with what we are together as Sudanese, I believe we can move with full confidence and be effective in those outside circles with which we identify. As Ambassador of Sudan and Minister of State for Foreign Affairs at a time when we were united and we could speak with one voice, I was proud to represent Sudan in Arab circles, and I was often chosen by Arab Ambassadors and Ministers to be their spokesman. I found no contradiction whatsoever in my role. But if I did not feel a sense of togetherness within myself as a Sudanese who knows who he is and proud of what he is, I would not be comfortable enough to represent my country with pride and dignity and therefore effectiveness. I could not be persuasive and I could not be convincing.

## The Scope of the National Dialogue

Let me now turn to issues pertaining to the work of this conference and make some procedural observations about the process and the scope. I think there is no doubt that the idea of this dialogue and its objectives is a noble one. It has been embraced by most of the people I have talked to, people who are committed to the interests of this country. It certainly promises to move the peace process forward, depending on how we conceive it, how we implement its objectives, and how we approach the substantive issues involved. Where there have been deep divisions of the kind we have been experiencing, there is always room for misunderstanding and misinterpretation. That is something I think we should guard against very carefully in order not to give anybody the opportunity to turn a positive step into a negative one. We should recognize that the call for the participation of the SPLM/A in this conference, well motivated as it is, cannot be heeded for practical reasons. I think that by combining a positive orientation with a degree of realism, we can do a lot more. We should conceive the work of this conference not as a dialogue between the warring parties, but as a discussion within one front, the internal framework. The best approach is for the internal forces to use this dialogue to unify their vision, develop a common ground on the complex issues in the conflict and the challenges facing the nation, and resolve how they can be addressed. With the results of the work and the degree of consensus that will have been reached, the government could then approach the SPLM/A to present those views as an advisory opinion, a guide or guidance to help the government negotiate a solution. That way, we would have reduced the equations to a more manageable dualism that can help enhance the peace process.

To the extent that we can even conceive of the SPLM/A being involved in these discussions, they would obviously have become part of the internal process. But to the extent that this dialogue is seen as an internal process that can help guide and facilitate the path in the subsequent discussions with the SPLM/A, it could be a very constructive step.

This means that the results of this dialogue cannot be conceived as the national will, as the solution to the problem, however successful it proves to be. The war is not among the factions sitting in this room; it is with factions outside this room. This dialogue can only help in bridging between the factions in this room that is the government or the nation inside, with the nation outside.

Since we are here talking very frankly, I would also say that while the Revolution for National Salvation has rejected past efforts that are associated with political parties whose objectives are partisan, there is also another aspect of building on the past that is constructive. We have had considerable experience with the search for peace, and some of our people, even as individuals have been associated with the peace process. One would hope that their experience and the wisdom they have acquired from that experience can be made use of in this dialogue. Since the committee's timetable is long enough to allow time to absorb varied contributions, one would hope that in the process, some of those individuals will be made use of and whatever lessons they have learned could be built upon in the process.

In this connection, it is also fair to say that it is only by having solutions that will ultimately be acceptable to the Sudanese people as a whole that we can expect to achieve lasting peace and stability. Therefore, as part of the work of this conference, perhaps at an earlier stage and of course at the stage of negotiations with the SPLM/A, we have to bear in mind the larger national constituency. Unless the Sudanese people accept the solutions developed, we could be generating counter activities that will threaten whatever achievements will have been made. Therefore, whatever the schedule for the dialogue, we should bear in mind that ultimately, we must bring on board all the Sudanese people in order for us to be truly united as one nation.

## Concluding Remarks

Permit me to end on a few concluding remarks. The question has often been posed, and I was personally asked by someone the other day: What do our brothers in the South really want? I cannot speak for our brothers in the South, but I can say that what any citizen wants is to be given the opportunity to be equal, fully identified with his nation, proud to be a citizen, to have a sense of belonging and to participate on equal footing in the affairs of his country. If we are genuinely guided by the fact that this is the goal of every individual Sudanese then I believe we will free ourselves to search constructively for the kinds of solutions that will enhance that goal.

In my discussions with the late Nazir Babo Nimir of the Missiriya Arabs, I asked him what the most important principle in his leadership as a tribal chief was? The gist of the answer he gave me is exactly what I had grown up knowing at home to be part of leadership values. In a conflict situation, as a leader, you must identify with the person who is farthest removed from you. Only by taking the side of the person who is far from you can you bridge between that person and your own group. Ultimately, it becomes not just a magnanimous, selfless way of administering justice, but also a way of serving the interests of those closer to you and therefore of yourself. This is the challenge that faces the leadership in Sudan. National leaders must rise above factions. Our leadership has been for so long viewed as reflective of factions rather than of the whole. Only by rising above factions and be seen by every Sudanese as the embodiment of the ideals of leadership with which we can all identify, feel that the person up there represents all of us, and be proud of that person as a reflection of all of us, only then can the leadership succeed in bringing us together and in making the Sudanese see a common purpose and a sense of true brotherhood and sisterhood; in other words, solidarity in mutual identification.

Let me say in conclusion once more how much I have appreciated the way I have been received, coming as a private citizen, wanting as a scholar or someone involved in research to come back and witness what was happening. As I said at the outset, I got a lot more than I had expected. One of the highlights of my being back here is the honor you have given me today, to address this August audience at a crossroads in the building of our nation. All I can say now is thank you for the opportunity. I wish you every success and Godspeed.

# 3 | Symposium on Self-Determination and Unity

During the second half of 2009, intellectuals, scholars, and political activists began to engage actively in debates concerning the likely outcome of the 2011 self-determination referendum in Southern Sudan. Time was running out and while most observers maintained a neutral position on the issue of unity and Southern secession, it was becoming clear that the cause of unity which was to be promoted during the interim period to make unity attractive to the Southern voters was failing and that the South would almost certainly vote for secession. The prospects of Sudan's partition began to ring alarm bells, and the possibility of salvaging the unity of the country suddenly became a matter of urgent attention for national, regional, and international organizations. Neutrality on the outcome of the referendum became increasingly challenged as people grappled with the search for ways of belatedly rescuing Sudan's unity.

As the organ of the United Nations most directly involved with the implementation of the Comprehensive Peace Agreement (CPA) and maintaining peace between the North and the South, the United Nations Mission in the Sudan (UNMIS) found itself in the midst of the debate on unity, self-determination, and the prospective partition of the country. It was in this context that the Information Section of UNMIS, in collaboration with a Sudanese think tank, Future Trends Foundation, organized the Symposium on Unity and Self-determination in Khartoum, November 2–3, 2009.

I was invited to give the keynote address, but knowing that the underlying objective was to advocate the cause of unity, and realizing that it was probably too late to make unity attractive to Southern voters in the referendum which was only two years away, I initially resisted participating in the symposium, but eventually gave into the persuasive persistence of the organizers. What follows is the text of my address broken up into subheadings for substantive flow and coherence.

## The Premise of the Keynote Address

It is a great pleasure and honor to have been invited to address this important meeting at this critical juncture in the history of our beleaguered country. I do so with humility, and needless to say, in my personal capacity and not as the Special Adviser of the United Nations Secretary-General on the Prevention of Genocide.

To be frank, this is an honor I was initially reluctant to accept for two reasons: First, I thought it was rather late in the process to be advocating making unity attractive as we approach the end of the interim period, during which unity was to be made attractive to the Southern voters in the self-determination referendum, an objective which, arguably, has not been achieved.

Second, the positions of the principal parties to the Comprehensive Peace Agreement (CPA) on the appropriate framework for unity seem too far apart to bridge in time to influence positively the referendum outcome.

In the end, and upon reflection, I agreed to participate, for the following reasons:

First, the seminar is co-sponsored by the United Nations Mission in Sudan (UNMIS), an organ of the organization which I serve.

Second, I reminded myself of a number of principles that have guided me over the years in my efforts to contribute to the cause of peace and unity in our country. Among these principles are:

Optimism is a vital tool for constructive engagement, while pessimism leads to a dead end.

Everyone is called upon to play a role in promoting the overriding goal of peace and unity and, although only a few eventually catch the limelight as the champions of the peace process, it is the cumulative effect of all the invisible contributions that bring about the desired outcome.

In light of the above principles, as long as there is time still left, efforts should be intensified to follow the age-old adage, "Better late than never." I have invested much of my adult life in promoting the cause of peace and unity in our country and it would be incongruous with my life-long commitments to give up because of the lateness of the hour.

## Participant-Observer's Standpoint

To put my views in context, it may be useful to highlight some personal positions in my role as a participant-observer in the painful history of postcolonial Sudan, in which I have lived my adult life.

Ever since I became politically conscious, and as those of you who have either read my writings or heard me talk on the subject will attest, I have been a strong supporter of unity, but on the basis of full equality and a shared sense of belonging to the nation, with pride and dignity for all citizens. I have also supported the right of self-determination for the South, not because I wanted the South to secede, but in order to motivate the national leadership, specifically in the North, to intensify efforts to create appropriate conditions that would make unity appeal to Southerners in a self-determination referendum.

My stance for conditional unity has deep roots in my background in the sensitive North-South border area of Abyei, whose bridging role the Abyei Protocol of the CPA acknowledges and upholds. It is indeed ironic that an area that has played such a vital role of bridging and reconciling the North and the South should have become a point of confrontation, hopefully now resolved by the outcome of the Hague Arbitration on the borders.

With this background, I have been honored to participate in many forums in promotion of peace and unity over the years, both within and outside Sudan, with a wide variety of think tanks, research institutions, and universities. Some of my efforts have been in partnership with world leaders, such as the then former president of Nigeria, Olusegun Obasanjo, and former president of the United States, Jimmy Carter, and some have been with institutions such as the U.S. Department of State, the United States Institute of Peace (USIP), and the Center for Strategic and International Studies (CSIS). I was also a member of an informal resource group convened by the Inter-Africa Group to support the Inter-Governmental Authority for Development (IGAD) peace initiative on Sudan, that eventually culminated in the CPA.

CSIS focused on developing a U.S.-Sudan policy that provided guidance for the mediation role the Bush Administration eventually played in partnership with others to end the North-South conflict through the CPA. I initially persuaded CSIS to include a number of Sudanese on the task force, but after attending a few earlier meetings, it was decided to exclude them in order not to distract the work of the task force by internal North-South confrontation. As co-chair and the only Sudanese on the CSIS task force, I played a role that was both conscious of my rather anomalous position as a Sudanese contributing to the shaping of U.S.-Sudan policy and strategic in providing the insights that eventually resulted in what I believe was a balanced report.

A critical element in that report was the need to reconcile two contrasting visions for the country from the North and the South through the "one country, two systems" formula that was later adopted by the CPA as the cornerstone of the agreement.

## Critical Questions to Be Addressed

People do not go to war to kill and risk being killed without a compelling cause; fighting is a measure of desperation, based on the assumption that all peaceful efforts have failed to remedy an intolerable situation. And although rights and wrongs are rarely equal, it is important to appreciate the concerns of both sides to a conflict and address them equitably.

The critical questions that therefore need to be asked and answered are: What were, and are, the wars in Sudan all about? To what extent has the CPA addressed and resolved the root causes of these wars? What challenges remain to be addressed to achieve sustained, genuinely comprehensive peace and unity throughout the country?

One word that is often used these days as a root cause of the regionally proliferating conflicts in Sudan, and is so widely applied to grievances throughout the country as to have lost its original focus on the South, is *marginalization*. What this means is that the Arab Center has monopolized power and national wealth to the exclusion of the peripheries in both the South and the North, which have thereby been marginalized.

There is, however, a deeper logic to stratification in Sudan and that is the extent to which the identity factors of one group, the Islamic Arab North, have been used to provide a national identity framework, which inevitably stratifies groups on those grounds and discriminates against both the non-Arab, non-Muslim Southern Sudanese, and the Muslim, but non-Arab, groups in the marginalized regions of the North.

Placed in its historical context, the Islamic-Arab assimilationist process in the North provided opportunities for self-enhancement to a respected status out of the denigrated categories of the non-Muslim blacks, while the South adopted an identity of resistance to assimilation engendered by the indignities of gross historical mistreatment.

Divisive subjective factors of self-identification eventually overshadowed the objective realities that embodied shared elements of identities, racial, ethnic, and cultural. This divisive identity framework was recognized, reinforced and consolidated by colonial policies, which, by introducing modern elements of gross inequalities into existing diversities, sewed the seeds of post-colonial conflicts.

Initially, this identity framework pitted the North against the South, seen as the most neglected and the most embittered by negative memories of painful history and continuing internal domination. Southern reaction was initially manifested in a secessionist war that united the whole North against the South and was eventually resolved through a compromise of autonomy for the South.

The unilateral abrogation of that agreement by the central government triggered the second war, but one in which the Sudan People's Liberation Movement and Army (SPLM/A) that championed the cause replaced secessionist objectives with a call for a New United Sudan, of full equality, without discrimination on the basis of race, ethnicity, religion, culture, or gender. By the same token, the vision of the New Sudan inevitably threatens the identity-based interests of the dominant group in the North, which can be expected to resist such a radical transformation.

This vision began to capture the imagination of the marginalized, largely non-Arab, regions and groups in the North, beginning with the Nuba and the Ingassana (Funj), and eventually extending to the Beja, the Darfurians, and even the Nubians to the far North.

The call for the New Sudan began to tear down the walls that had historically dichotomized the country into North and South. Even those in the North, who resist radical transformation towards a New Sudan, have made significant concessions, although a considerable gap has yet to be bridged.

## The Solutions in the CPA

The CPA has addressed the national identity crisis between the North and the South by granting the South autonomy during the interim period and the right to opt out of unity through a referendum to be held at the end of that period.

It did not, however, resolve the national identity crisis comprehensively, although it lays a foundation for the democratic transformation of the governance system in the whole country.

Although the CPA stipulated that efforts be exerted during the interim period to make unity attractive to the Southern voters in the self-determination referendum, the "one country, two systems" formula that was aimed at reconciling the two contrasting visions for the country paradoxically entrenched the differences between the two, inadvertently favoring Southern secession, and leaving the crisis of marginalization in the North unresolved.

The CPA was intended to provide not only a framework for the democratic transformation of the governance system in the country, but also principles for resolving the regional conflicts in the North. Quite the contrary, it has ironically become a tool for containment by the ruling National Congress Party (NCP), which now doubles as the government of the North and the dominant party in the Government of National Unity.

Considering that those who stand for the New Sudan in the North are either members or allies of the SPLM, an independent South under the leadership of the SPLM can be expected to continue to support their cause. Southern dissidents, too, are likely to continue to look to the North for support, especially if the North and the South are antagonistic towards one another. By the same token, the prospects of reunification in the event of the New Sudan emerging in the North and the South cannot be ruled out.

It is obvious, therefore, that the secession of the South would not necessarily end the conflicts in Sudan without resolving the national identity crisis in the North and establishing an equitable governance system in the South. Likewise, the prospects for the unity of the country do not necessarily cease with the independence of the South.

## The Challenges for the Nation

For all these reasons, it is urgently important to assess the situation and reflect on what can still be done at this late hour to resolve the crisis in the country comprehensively, not only to implement the CPA with credibility and genuine goodwill, but also to resolve the crisis in Darfur and prospective conflicts in other regions of the North, building on the principles laid down in the CPA, especially those enshrined in the protocols on the two areas, Southern Kordofan and Blue Nile. This could generate a surprisingly positive environment in the country and enhance the prospects of salvaging the threat of disintegration throughout the country.

At this juncture, the country faces pressing challenges with two sets of critical questions:

First, can anything be done at this late hour to make unity attractive to Southern votes in the self-determination referendum?

Second, what can be done to anticipate the worst-case scenarios in the event of the South voting for independence and to prepare constructive remedial responses?

Making unity attractive requires action on both material and moral grounds. Material action would require making peace dividends immediately visible: embarking on massive construction of roads and other infrastructural projects; providing social services to the people, particularly in the areas of health and education; generating rural development activities; and sending messages of goodwill, genuine change of heart, and readiness to address the grievances that have divided the country since independence.

Moral areas of action call for sending a clear message that Sudan is embarking on a genuine and sincere search for the common ground, based on what unites rather than on what divides. Subjective self-identification has led to a self-enhancing distortion of the objective realities that reflect more in common and provide a sound ground for a uniting sense of national identity as Sudanese. Proclamations by national leaders in that direction could immediately create a climate conducive to a sense of a common cause and a new ground for prospective unity.

However, unity should not be seen as an end in itself or as the only option in the pursuit of human fulfillment and dignity. A vote for Southern independence, therefore, confronts the nation with challenges that must be addressed constructively in the interest of both North and South. This should mean making the process of partition as harmonious as possible and laying the foundation for peaceful and cooperative coexistence and continued interaction. Practical measures should be taken to ensure continued sharing of such vital resources as oil and water, encouraging cross-border trade, protecting freedom of movement, residence and employment across the borders, and leaving the door open for periodically revisiting the prospects of reunification.

## Concluding Remarks

As a country, Sudan is confronted with an extraordinary dilemma: Sudanese and the world would prefer Sudan to remain united, but the contrasting visions for the country seem too far apart to be bridged.

The question the Sudanese must answer at this late hour is: What is the most important consideration for them, building on the self-perceptions of identity that both distort the objective realities of the country and divide the nation, or searching for a common ground and a restructuring of a uniting national identity framework.

If the latter is agreed to be the case, then action needs to be taken immediately to not only open a new page, but to also make it credibly and conspicuously evident for all to see.

The elements of such a new dispensation should be:

Decentralization throughout the country in which all regions of the country, North and South, enjoy self-rule similar to the system accorded the South, short of the right to secede.

Equitable representation in the Government of National Unity, with due consideration to proportional representation based on demographic weight, but with due safeguards for minorities.

A declaration of principles for full equality of citizenship, without discrimination on the basis of race, ethnicity, culture, religion, or gender.

The creation of mechanisms and institutions for ensuring the immediate implementation of these policies, with the objective of showing visible results, if possible before the referendum in the South.

Engaging the international community both to oversee the credibility of implementation and to support these last-minute efforts to salvage and promote the essential principles of making unity attractive to the Southern voters in the self-determination referendum.

Working with all concerned not only to advocate the cause of unity, but also to prepare to counter the negative consequences of separation, and promote peaceful coexistence and cooperation between the North and an independent South.

If, as I have argued, both the North and the South will continue to face internal challenges in the event of Southern independence, and if, as I have also argued, the prospects for reunification under the right conditions cannot be ruled out, and, further, if aspirations for unity are widely shared, as appears to be the case, then an expedited search for genuinely comprehensive peace and unity becomes urgently compelling. Consequently, the referendum and the possible independent vote should not be viewed as the end of the road, the search for harmonious and productive relations among Sudan's many component parts is surely an ongoing process that will continue to challenge Sudanese on all sides as the nation searches for an inclusive identity and common sense of purpose rooted in their shared destiny.

# 4 | Update on Developments

This note builds on the findings and observations from my recent visit to Sudan and Ethiopia. Sudan is confronted with multiple crises that, if not constructively managed, could explode in a genocidal catastrophe. These crises are not only reflected in the increasingly tense relations between North and South, as the self-determination referendum of 2011 approaches, but also in interethnic conflicts within the North and the South. Apprehensions about the implications of Southern independence are rising not only within Sudan, but also in the subregion, at the level of the African continent, and internationally. Given the large numbers of Southerners residing in the North, a hostile partition could result in genocidal atrocities reminiscent of the Indian-Pakistan partition.

Even if the South secedes, the quest for a New Sudan of nondiscrimination on the grounds of race, ethnicity, religion, culture, or gender, which the Sudan People's Liberation Movement and Army (SPLM/A) has championed, will most likely be pursued by the non-Arab groups in the North, including in Southern Kordofan, Blue Nile, the Beja in the East, several groups in Darfur, and even the Nubians bordering Egypt in the far North. These groups would probably seek support from the independent South. But if the South were to support liberation movements in the North, Khartoum would most certainly react by using the ethnic tensions in the South to undermine the Government of Southern Sudan (GoSS), create chaos, and render the South ungovernable. It is therefore in the mutual interest of all the factions in Sudan and others concerned to find a common ground for a genuinely comprehensive peace within the framework of national unity, or make the process of partition as peaceful, harmonious, and cooperative as possible.

Although the visit to Sudan was not a mission in the normal sense, I held intensive discussions in all the three areas I visited, and was able to acquire significant insights and draw some conclusions on the prevailing situation in the country. The following is a summary of my findings:

First, there was a wide-spread apprehension about the self-determination referendum in the South, which is predicted to result in Southern secession. The view shared by many in Sudan and in Africa generally is that Southern secession would be disastrous for the South, for the subregion, and even for Africa.

Second, there are widespread allegations that this awesome prediction is, in significant part, orchestrated by Khartoum in order to promote a self-fulfilling prophecy of a South Sudan that would not be capable of governing itself, is almost certain to be a failed state, and would be a burden to the region and the international community. Hardly any effort is made to analyze the factors that might account for this predicted disaster and what can be done to avert it and help the South succeed, in the interest of regional peace, security, and stability.

Third, an aspect of the concerns about the future of an independent South is that, overwhelmingly, the emphasis is being placed on the glass being mostly empty, with hardly any attempt made to appreciate what has so far been achieved against formidable odds, which are deeply rooted in historic neglect and the devastations of half a century of war.

Fourth, ironically, while the prospective secession of the South is dreaded, no commensurate attention is being given to the changes needed at the central level to make the prospects of national unity attractive or at least palatable to the South.

Fifth, there has been a tendency to see the crisis in Darfur in isolation of the crises in the South and conflicts in other regions of the North. The one word often given as the root cause of these proliferating regional conflicts is the marginalization of non-Arab regions by the Islamist Arab Center.

The foregoing findings lead to the following correlative observations and recommendations:

First, the predicted disastrous consequences of Southern secession have the ominous implication that it should better not be allowed, which would mean dishonoring the CPA. Already, controversies over the conduct and results of the census, preparations for the 2010 national elections, the reluctance to implement the Abyei Protocol and the arbitration award, and arrangements for the referendums in the South and in Abyei were sending serious signals that the CPA would not be credibly implemented and might even be blatantly dishonored. If this were to happen, the South would almost certainly take up arms again, perhaps jointly with the other marginalized non-Arab regions of the North. There are already indications of an arms race between the CPA partners, which points to the potential for the resumption of hostilities. To avoid a return to war, the CPA must be honored and fully implemented.

Second, the failures of the GoSS should be identified and analyzed to provide a basis for corrective measures to prevent the anticipated disaster. If the problem of the GoSS is a lack of governance capacity, then all concerned should assist in providing or reinforcing that capacity, with immediate effect.

Third, in order to enhance the capacity of the South to govern itself, it is important to appreciate what has already been accomplished in establishing the institutions of government at the level of the GoSS and in the Southern states. Tribal leaders also have a largely unutilized potential for maintaining law and order in the rural areas, which was effectively used by the colonial administration and have been undermined by postcolonial policies and the impact of war. They too can be supported and strengthened to promote peace and security in the areas under their influence.

Fourth, although reforming the national governance framework to make unity attractive is a formidable task for which there is precious little time, dramatic changes to generate the process of democratic transformation envisioned by the CPA might still improve the prospects for national unity. This could be done by immediately

putting in place in all the regions of the North a system of autonomy similar to that of the South, with equitable sharing of power
at the national level.

Fifth, to correct the tendency to isolate the Darfur crisis and other
regional conflicts in the North from the situation in the South and
to address the marginalization of the peripheries by the Arab-dom-
inated Center, the country should go beyond the "one country, two
systems" formula of the CPA and adopt a confederal model of "one
country, multiple systems". While there is good reason to be concerned about the divisiveness of multiplicity, the currently prevailing "one country, two systems" model is proving to be more
divisive than a basis for unity, as initially intended. The "one country, multiple systems" model would facilitate crosscutting alliances
that would provide a basis for democratic transformation and reinforce national unity. Harmonious interaction among the peoples
of the various regions could incrementally generate a process of
national integration that would eventually result in the consolida-
tion of national unity toward a "one country, one system" model
which is the ideal.

Abyei continues to be a challenge for peace, unity, and stability in
the country. Now that the NCP can be said to have successfully challenged the ABC border demarcation, and in light of the Abyei arbitration award, which clearly balanced the interests of the North and the
South regarding the borders, and reaffirmed the traditional grazing
rights of the Missiriya, the parties to the CPA must demonstrate
mutual goodwill and cooperation in ensuring the credible implementation of the tribunal's decision. The demonstration of such states-
manship would go a long way in promoting peace, conciliation, and
cooperation between the Dinka and the Missiriya. National leaders
must be seen to be leaders of all Sudanese and not of factions. They
must also protect all the citizens without prejudice or favor. The hor-
rific destruction that was inflicted on Abyei in March 2008 must never
be allowed to happen again. The Government of National Unity
(GoNU) and the NCP in particular must bear the responsibility for
ensuring that peace and security prevail in the area and that Abyei can

once again play the bridging role it has historically played between the North and the South, as the CPA indeed acknowledges and upholds.

Whatever the outcome of the 2011 referendum in the South, viewed within a dynamic mid- to long-term frame, the cause of unity can continue to be pursued. After all, unity and separation are varying degrees of relationships that could be strengthened or weakened by the qualitative factors involved. Making unity attractive has the material dimension that would require implementing quick impact projects of socio-economic development in the areas of infrastructure, especially those linking the North and the South, and social services in such areas as health, education, and employment, especially of youth. But even more important is the moral dimension which means dramatically creating a national identity framework that would remove from the public domain factors that have in the past provided a basis for discrimination and fostering a common sense of belonging to the nation on equal footing as citizens.

Nevertheless, the likelihood, even the probability, of the South opting for secession cannot be ruled out and should be approached constructively by anticipating the crisis points and addressing them to promote peaceful coexistence and cooperation between North and South Sudan as neighbors with deeply rooted bonds of history. Freedom of movement across the borders, residence, employment, and the sharing of such vital resources as oil and water, can be negotiated to mutual benefit. With the prospects of democratic transformation toward a reconstructed Sudan of nondiscrimination in both the North and the South, and with mutual trust developed through cooperative association, the possibility of reunification should not be dismissed and perhaps be explicitly provided in the articles of friendly partition.

Toward these objectives, the United Nations, in close cooperation with the African Union, the Inter-Governmental Authority for Development, and all stakeholders in the CPA must remain vigilantly engaged. With a sense of urgency, they should help ongoing dialogue or consultations on the vital issues involved, and mobilize the support needed to implement quick-impact unity projects and address some of the anticipated problem areas to preempt any negative consequences of Southern independence.

It must be born in mind that the failure to honor the CPA could be catastrophic. Experience has shown that the outbreak of war in response to violation of peace accords is often spontaneous and uncontrollable, while the negative consequences of secession can be anticipated and prevented. Given the level of mistrust, the bitterness associated with protracted wars of identities, the easy availability of sophisticated weapons, and the tensions associated with the breakup of the country, if hostilities were to resume, the situation would almost certainly become genocidal, with atrocities at a mass scale. This must be prevented—and the time to take preventive measures is now.

# 5 | Ten Principles on Negotiations

Negotiations with third-party mediation are the counterpart to violent confrontation. Since independence, Sudan has twice alternated between devastating violent conflicts and negotiations leading to the peaceful resolution of the conflicts. The seventeen-year war (1955–1972) was ended by the Addis Ababa Agreement and the twenty-two-year war (1983–2005) ended with the Comprehensive Peace Agreement. The search for durable peace and the prospects for achieving genuine consensual unity will continue to require an ongoing process of negotiations into the foreseeable future.

I see negotiation and the closely related field of diplomacy as essentially management of human relations involving individuals, groups, or nations. Some people would argue that conflict is the normal state of human interaction and that it is futile to try to prevent or resolve conflicts; the most that can be done is managing conflicts. This can only be valid if it is understood to mean that grounds for conflict exist in normal human relations and that the *occurrence* of conflict is therefore normal. If it means that conflict is the normal *pattern* of life, then I would consider that position both empirically questionable and normatively ambiguous. Far from seeing conflict as the normal state of human interaction, I believe that people are more apt to cooperate and harmonize their incompatible or potentially conflictual positions, and that conflict is in fact a crisis that signifies a breakdown in the normal pattern of behavior. In this sense, conflict involves a collision of incompatible positions resulting from a failure to regulate, reconcile or harmonize the differences. In the normal course of events, society is structured around fundamental values and norms that guide behavior and regulate relations so as to avoid a destructive collision of interests or positions. If people observe the principles of the normative code, which they generally do, the normal pattern would be one of relative cooperation and mutual accommodation, even in a competitive framework. To call that state one of conflict would be to put a negative value judgment on positive motivations and endeavors, and on a relatively high degree of success in peaceful interaction.

Even more important than strict empirical interpretation would be the normative implications of holding conflict the normal state of human existence, which would tend to foster a disposition that is fundamentally adversarial, suspicious, and conflictual. The extent to which members in a community or group reflect this disposition may depend in large measure on the culture and its normative code, defined as a set of shared and enduring meanings, values, and beliefs that characterizes national, ethnic, or other groups and orient their behavior.

Culture itself is a product of education, both formal and informal, through which the norms of behavior that a society has developed over a long period of time are inculcated from early childhood and passed on from generation to generation. The family is the institutional foundation of education, and, in particular, of the inculcation of basic cultural values. And yet, despite the pivotal role of the family and the culture in shaping values, attitudes, and operational techniques in human relations, individuals differ even within a family in their understanding, appreciation, and application of the values involved. It is this combination of the collective cultural conditioning and the individual inclination to absorb, accept, and apply what is acquired that gives significance to personal experiences as particular applications of values, customs, and techniques of conflict resolution and diplomacy within a specific cultural framework. As a challenge to grossly inequitable order, conflict may be a positive quest for reform.

It is important to emphasize that the objective is not merely to resolve a conflict, but to resolve it in a mutually satisfactory manner. This means addressing the root causes and observing such fundamental norms as justice and human dignity. In other words, where change is urgently needed, the status quo cannot simply be supported for the sake of harmony and peaceful interaction.

Conflict in this context can be defined as a situation of interaction involving two or more parties in which actions in pursuit of conflicting objectives or interests result in varying degrees of discord. The principal dichotomy is between normally harmonious and cooperative relations and a disruptive adversarial confrontation, culminating at its worst in high-intensity violence. On the basis of this definition, conflict resolution is a normative concept aimed at reconciling, harmonizing, or managing incompatible interests by fostering a process of institutionalized peaceful interaction. Conflict resolution envisages strategies aimed at restoring or establishing the normal state of affairs and raising the level of peaceful, harmonious, cooperative, constructive, and productive interaction.

The achievement of peace and reconciliation becomes a common objective, but one that is only possible if both sides feel that the solution proposed is indeed in the mutual interest. Since both were prepared to enter into conflict in the first place, it means that each must have a subjective view of right and wrong that gives them some degree of right and places some degree of wrong on the opposing party. These subjective perspectives cannot be ignored when negotiation takes place or when proposals are made for resolving a conflict, even though they need not and should not be allowed to have too much influence on such processes. Ultimately, while there is indeed a hierarchy of rights and wrongs in resolving disputes through negotiations, there should be no absolute winner or loser.

If one comes from a culture, a society, or a family in which unity, harmony, and cooperation are highly valued, then the discord of conflict becomes a disruption that is destabilizing not only to the community, but also intrinsically to the individual. And if one assumes further that in any conflict there are contributing factors for which both sides share responsibility, albeit in varying degrees, then the degree of uncertainty involved must create a sense of shared responsibility for properly tutored or nurtured members of the community. The desire to normalize the situation and restore amicable relations therefore becomes as much a societal as it is an individual objective.

## Expounding the Principles

The proposed principles on negotiation should be seen in the context of the normative framework outlined above. These principles derive from personal experiences and are rooted in values, norms and mores that emanate from a specific African family and cultural background among the Dinka of Sudan. They cover experiences in interpersonal relations, third-party mediation, and diplomatic negotiations, with overlaps. Although personal and rooted in the Dinka, Sudanese, and African cultural contexts, they represent values that can claim universal validity, despite cross-cultural variations on the details and their applicability.

Principle One: Rights and wrongs, though seldom equal, are rarely one-sided. Even when you feel sure that you are in the right, you must not only strive to fit yourself into the shoes of the other side, but must also make the other side recognize that you are genuinely interested in his or her point of view.

Principle Two: It is unhealthy to keep grievances "in the stomach" or "in the heart." *Talking It Out*, the title of a book I wrote on the theme, is not only the best way to resolve differences or grievances, but is also essential for one's mental and even physical health. Often "what is not said is what divides," to use the words of an article I wrote on that theme.

Principle Three: Face-saving is crucial to resolving conflicts. One must avoid saying anything that is humiliating to the other side, and, where possible, it is advisable to show deference, even to an adversary, provided it is not cheap flattery.

Principle Four: It is important to listen very carefully and allow the other party to say all that she or he considers significant or relevant. Resolving differences is not a game of wits or cleverness, but of addressing the genuine concerns of the parties in conflict. In Dinka folktales, the cleverness of the fox eventually turns against the fox. Ideally, resolutions must have an element of give and take, although the distribution should be proportional to the equations of the rights and wrongs involved. In assessing the outcome of a negotiated settlement of a dispute, it is unwise to boast of victory, for that implies defeat for the other side and therefore an unsatisfactory outcome.

Principle Five: Historical memory of the relations gives depth to the perspectives of the parties and the issues involved, but one must avoid aggravating the situation with negative recollections and emphases and should instead reinforce constructive dialogue with positive recollections or interpretations of past events, without, of course, distorting the facts.

Principle Six: The mediator must be seen to be impartial, but where there is reason to believe that he or she is closer to one side in whatever capacity, the mediator must reach out to the more distant party. However, this should not be at the cost of fairness to the party closer to the mediator. Impartiality does not mean having no position on the issues in dispute, even though voicing opinions should be carefully coached to maximize the bridging role and promote mutual understanding.

Principle Seven: The mediator must listen very patiently to both parties, and even when there are obvious flaws in what is said, the mediator must appear to give due weight to each party's point of view. The popular view that in the indigenous African system of dispute settlement, people sat under the tree and talked until they reached a consensus reflects a broadly shared African normative behavior. Where explaining the opponent's view on a specific issue might facilitate the bridging process, the mediator should intercede to offer an explanation as part of consensus building.

Principle Eight: While the wisdom of words and the ability to persuade are important, leverage is pivotal. This means that the mediator must have, or be believed to have, the ability to support the process with incentives or threats of negative consequences, according to the equations of the responsibility for the success or failure of the negotiations. In the past, among the Dinka, spiritual powers of divine leadership provided the required leverage. In the modern context, influencing the balance of power to create a "mutually hurting stalemate" and help advance the process of "ripening for resolution," to borrow the famous words of the renowned scholar of conflict analysis, William Zartman, is part of the leverage that can effectively facilitate the mediator's task.

Principle Nine: Diplomatic negotiations combine elements of both interpersonal relations and third-party mediation in that the negotiator represents his or her government and in a sense combines negotiating with mediating between the respective governments involved. Discretion and creativity in adapting the official position to the dynamics of the situation with a degree of flexibility is critical to the prospects of successful bridging.

Principle Ten: While the tendency of the negotiators is to see the outcome of their efforts in terms of winning or losing, especially for domestic consumption, the desired outcome should be one in which neither side sees itself as a total winner or loser, except where the rights and wrongs involved are incontrovertibly clear. The win-win formula should be the objective and whatever the equations of winning or losing in the mediated or negotiated outcome, as noted in Principle Four, neither side should boast about winning and by implication humiliate the other side as a loser. There must be a degree of parity in both sides winning or losing.

## Balancing the Universal with the Particular

The principles presented above do not claim to be a panacea. Quite the contrary, they reflect a particular emotional value system that may be more relative than universal. On the other hand, it would also be presumptuous and even hazardous to assume that these are universal, scientifically proven negotiation techniques that are applicable to all situations and cross-cultural contexts. A case can, of course, be made for expert knowledge in negotiation and there is a particular role to be played by individuals with such expertise. But to be effective a synergy between universal techniques and culturally specific methods need to be developed.

In Sudan, chiefs and elders known as *ajaweed* in the North but with varying titles throughout the country are usually made effective use of to mediate in intertribal conflicts. Indeed, most tribal conflicts, which are pervasive throughout the country, are resolved by these traditional mediators, for the most part illiterate but endowed with indigenous knowledge and wisdom. When one recalls that the number of colonial administrators who controlled that vast country of nearly a million square miles was relatively small, it is easy to see how they made effective use of traditional leaders to maintain law and order, peace and security throughout the rural areas. Failure to use this indigenous capacity accounts for much of the intertribal warfare and criminal violence that has been the lot of the postcolonial administration in Sudan. This must be reversed if Sudan is to enhance its full capacity for promoting peace, security, and stability throughout the country.

This chapter is adapted from Francis M. Deng, "The Sudan: Education, Culture, and Negotiations," in Even in Chaos: Education in Times of Emergency, ed. Kevin M. Cahill, M.D. (New York: Fordham University Press, 2010).

During the first half of 2010, the position of the international community on the situation in Sudan has developed quite constructively in several ways. A consensus has emerged in support of the full implementation of the CPA. This includes holding the referenda in the South and in Abyei as scheduled and respecting the choice of the people, whether for unity or for partition. Accordingly, the measures needed for the conduct of the referenda, such as the demarcation of the borders and the establishment of the referenda commissions, voter registration, and other procedural requirements should be carried out diligently, credibly, and transparently.

It is also widely agreed that the parties should negotiate postreferenda arrangements on both North-South and Dinka-Missiriya (Abyei) relations to ensure not only that the referenda are carried out peacefully, but also that durable peaceful relations for the future are guaranteed.

The international community has also realized the importance of bringing Darfur back into the complex web of Sudan's interconnected regional conflicts. Since the outbreak of the Darfur conflict in 2003, the tendency in the international community has been to see it in isolation from the situation in the South and conflict situations in other regions of the North. In reality, Darfur is only the latest in a series of regional conflicts that began in the South in the 1950s, extended to the North in the mid-1980s into the regions of the Nuba

Mountains, Blue Nile, and the Beja, and eventually Darfur, with the common cause being the marginalization of these peripheral areas by the Center. This center-periphery dichotomy corresponds to an Arab-African divide that is more perceptional than factual.

The report of the African Union High-Level Panel on Darfur—which was chaired by Thabo Mbeki, former president of South Africa, and whose mandate has now been expanded to include the implementation of the CPA—has restored the proper balance to see the conflict in Darfur in the national context, including the connection with the CPA and the South. These complex sets of considerations are also leading the Sudanese themselves and the international community to the conclusion that the debate over the unity and partition of Sudan does not end with the Southern self-determination referendum. Even if the South were to opt for secession, they will remain closely connected to the North—physically, economically, socially, and culturally. Even more pertinently they will continue to identify themselves with the grievances of the marginalized regions of the North and their struggle for the realization of a New Sudan of nondiscrimination on the bases of race, ethnicity, religion, culture, and gender. Should that vision be realized, the basis for national unity would have been established.

For that reason, it would be wiser to see a vote for secession as an interim arrangement that should leave the door open for reunification. By the same token, some form of association that would keep in place the strings of unity and close cooperation should be established. That would not only keep the vision of unity alive, but would also facilitate a climate of goodwill and peaceful partition, should that be the outcome of the self-determination referendum in the South.

Abyei also offers a similar challenge between the North and the South. If the Southern referendum were to take place before Abyei's and the South voted for unity, I would have advocated a special status for Abyei within unity. The question then is whether a special status for Abyei within the framework of Southern secession is possible. The objective would be to give both parties a positive connection to Abyei and negotiate a partnership aimed at giving Abyei the status of belonging to both, to continue to be a dynamic link between the North and the South. The Dinka-Missiriya Council for Peace and Development, which I proposed during the CPA negotiations, would provide a grassroots institutional base for this partnership. In order for such an arrangement to work, it must give the Dinka and the Missirya clear and tangible mutual benefits to make it an attractive point of contact, interaction and cooperation between the North and the South. It must also give both north and south a clear benefit in Abyei's status.

It has always been my view that there is much more in common among the Sudanese that transcends the North-South divide than they realize. But, perhaps for the same reason, there is a tendency to emphasize what divides, which gives extremists on both sides slogans for claiming legitimacy for their divisive agendas. It is ironic that the vision of unity within a New Sudan should come from the South, which has historically been associated with secession. It is also opportune that this vision has captured the imagination of the marginalized regions of the North that constitute the majority. The statesman-like challenge for the leadership at the Center is to respond positively to the demands of the overwhelming majority of the Sudanese people for a New Sudan of full equality, without discrimination on any grounds. This is too lofty and compelling a vision for any leader deserving national and international legitimacy to resist. The only practical consideration is how to plan for a dispensation that protects the interests of the now dominant minority, as it cedes power to the now subordinated majority. To foster national unity and unified sense of purpose, magnanimity is required from both those ceding control and those called upon to take over and chart the destiny of the nation.

The Institute for International Humanitarian Affairs (IIHA) offers students of all levels an academic base for the study of humanitarian aid. At a time when terrorism and war are at the forefront of international affairs, the Institute is committed to training humanitarian workers to adapt within diverse crisis situations by giving them the critical skills needed to operate effectively in unfamiliar and often dangerous situations.

Through multidisciplinary coursework in humanitarian assistance, negotiations, and disaster management, offered at both the graduate and undergraduate levels, the IIHA trains students to find practical solutions to crises through the initiation of discourse and cooperation. The IIHA trains students for careers in the humanitarian field by combining an advanced academic approach with the shared practical field experience of both students and faculty.

To further supplement our mission, the IIHA frequently holds symposia, panel discussions, and networking events with humanitarian professionals. Its International Humanitarian Affairs book series and occasional papers are widely used both at the university and in the field. We provide consultation on humanitarian affairs to the Fordham community and to the international development community at large. Through these contacts, the IIHA creates a unique bridge between academia and front-line humanitarian efforts worldwide.